Contents

Making choices 4

Parents and children 6

The issue of sex 8

The abortion question 10

Euthanasia – the big debate 12

Discrimination 14

The right to privacy 16

The question of lying 18

Blowing the whistle 20

The drug problem 22

The aims of punishment 24

The rights and wrongs of aid 26

Morals at work 28

The right to protest 30

Tampering with nature 32

People before profit? 34

It's not my fault! 36

The rights and wrongs of war 38

Terrorism 40

The value of nature 42

Glossary 44

Contacts and helplines 46

Further reading 47

Index 48

Introduction

Throughout your life you will face many serious issues that you will need to take a **moral** stand on. You'll need to decide what to do or what to think. For example, whether you think **abortion** is right or wrong, or whether terrorism can be justified. There are different views on what is right and wrong and you may have to choose between them. This book introduces some of today's key issues and the many ways of thinking about them.

Making choices

The way we live involves making choices. Some of these choices are **moral** ones – decisions about the rights and wrongs of what we should do or what we should think. Let's say you are in trouble at school but can get out of it by blaming someone else. You have a choice to make. Do you tell the truth by admitting you did it? Or do you blame an innocent student and let them be punished? The choice you make will say something about how you want to live your life. On the one hand, you are prepared to lie to protect your own interests and allow an innocent person to be punished; on the other, you are prepared to admit your guilt and accept your punishment.

Absolutely right or wrong

Many people try to follow principles or rules that give them a clear-cut direction as to how to act or think when they are faced with making moral choices. Religious rules provide this kind of direction. Christians follow ten Commandments, rules stating principles such as 'Thou shalt not kill'. When people have such principles, they may believe they should follow them through in every situation. If you follow the principle that it's always wrong to kill another human being, then you would be against abortion, euthanasia, suicide and killing in war.

Some religions insist that it is wrong to have medical treatment of some kinds, because if God gave you a certain condition then there must be a reason for it. However, for many people, such as this girl who has had a heart **transplant**, medical intervention is the only way of keeping them alive.

Choosing between principles

However, following an absolute principle does not always work. We are often faced with having to decide between principles or duties that conflict with one another. You have to decide which one to follow. This is what we call a 'moral **dilemma**'.

RIGHT OR WRONG?

Alexander Gray

Heinemann
LIBRARY

www.heinemann.co.uk
Visit our website to find out more information about **Heinemann Library** books.

To order:
 Phone 44 (0) 1865 888066
Send a fax to 44 (0) 1865 314091
Visit the Heinemann Bookshop at www.heinemann.co.uk to browse our catalogue and order online.

First published in Great Britain by Heinemann Library, Halley Court, Jordan Hill, Oxford OX2 8EJ, a division of Reed Educational and Professional Publishing Ltd. Heinemann is a registered trademark of Reed Educational & Professional Publishing Limited.

OXFORD MELBOURNE AUCKLAND JOHANNESBURG BLANTYRE
GABORONE IBADAN PORTSMOUTH NH (USA) CHICAGO

Designed by Tinstar Design (www.tinstar.co.uk)
Originated by Ambassador Litho Ltd
Printed in Hong Kong/China

ISBN 0 431 03540 7   (hardback)   ISBN 0 431 03547 4   (paperback)
05 03 02 01   05 04 03 02 01
10 9 8 7 6 5 4 3 2 1   10 9 8 7 6 5 4 3 2 1

British Library Cataloguing in Publication Data
Gray, Alexander
    Right or wrong. – (What's at issue?)
    1. Right or wrong – Juvenile literature 2. Immorality –
    Juvenile literature
    I. Title
    170

Acknowledgements
The Publishers would like to thank the following for permission to reproduce photographs:
Amnesty International: p20; Corbis: pp12, 16, 19, 21, 24, 29, Jeff Kowalsky p13, Christian Liewig p14, David Reed p20, Peter Turnley p26, Howard Davies p27, Joseph Sohm pp30, 38, Charles Philip p42; Heinemann: p36; Rex Features: pp4, 17, 22, 23, 37, 39, 41, David Hancock p5, Justin Williams p10, Peter Brooker p11, Richard Gardner p25, Brendan Beirne p31, J Sutton Hibbert p32, Nick Cobbins p33, Sipa Press p40, Anthony Upton p43; Tony Stone Images: p18, Jon Riley p6, Penny Tweedie p7, Mark Romine p8, David Stewart p9, Walter Hodges p15, David Young-Wolff p28, Tim Brown p34, Ben Osborne p35

Cover photograph: Photofusion (Ian Simpson).

Our thanks to Julie Turner (School Counsellor, Banbury School, Oxfordshire) for her comments in the preparation of this book.

Every effort has been made to contact copyright holders of any material reproduced in this book. Any omissions will be rectified in subsequent printings if notice is given to the Publisher.

Any words appearing in the text in bold, **like this**, are explained in the Glossary.

Say, for example, you have to choose between following your principle of never telling a lie or telling a lie to save a friend's life. The chances are you will regard protecting your friend's life as more important than not telling lies. In this case doing something 'wrong' (telling a lie) is justified because it brings about good consequences.

The consequences are what count

In many cases we decide what to do or think because of what we believe the effects or consequences will be. We may feel that the right choice is the one that would bring about the most good for the most people. For example, criminals are imprisoned to stop them committing more crimes. It is generally believed that this will bring about the most good for the most people.

Many issues, such as euthanasia, raise serious moral questions and cause great debates that keep them in the news.

There will be times when you have to make a difficult choice based on what could happen as a result of your decision. Let's say that you have a friend who is obsessed with her weight and keeps going on about being too fat. She loses a lot of weight and seems to have no energy. You are worried and talk to her. She confides in you that she has been on a severe diet which she is keeping secret from other people, and is planning to get even thinner. You are worried she may be **anorexic**. You have to decide between keeping her secret, even though her health is at risk, or telling someone who can help her. If you do tell, you may lose her trust and perhaps her friendship. What would you do?

Parents and children

Most parents and step-parents want to do the best they can for the children in their care. They try to provide a home, food and clothing. They make sure you go to school and do your homework. They try to keep you healthy and look after you when you are sick. They teach you the difference between right and wrong and protect you against harm. It all sounds simple. So why are there so many problems and arguments between children and parents?

Children's rights

You have a **right** to your own opinions and to have a say in decisions that affect your life – who you want to be friends with, what you choose to study, where you go on holiday, what clothes you like. Some parents find it hard to let children

Parent and child – it can be a great relationship. But it's impossible to have a completely perfect family life all the time because loving relationships always involve a certain amount of conflict and some give and take.

find their own way, and try to impose their views on their children. Young people should be given enough freedom to work things out for themselves. Their thoughts and feelings need to be taken into account and not simply ignored.

Becoming a young adult is a difficult time – there are all sorts of pressures on you at school and in your personal life. You need as much support and encouragement as you can get. Parents can help – but they might need a little understanding and support themselves.

Parent problems

Parents are only human. There's no single correct way of being a parent. No one can train you to be a perfect parent. Parents have their off-days when they are bad-tempered and unreasonable. Sometimes they have worries at work or money difficulties. Maybe they are facing a difficult **dilemma**. If they are separated or divorced, they may worry about who should look after the children and how often the other parent should see them? If they need or want to work, who should look after the children? The problem for these parents is making sure their children's best interests are cared for while also living their own lives.

Parents may know best. They have had more experience of life and the world than their children and they may be able to see problems that a younger person cannot. But conflicts should be discussed in a positive way. If at all possible, parents and children should talk things through to find a compromise or 'middle way' that they can both live with. If parents and children respect each other's views and opinions, family life may not prove to be such a rocky ride.

GROUNDED!

A teenage girl is told by her mum to come home from a party by midnight. The girl has such a good time that she misses her lift and gets home at 3am on the back of a stranger's motorbike. Her mum is angry and grounds her for a month. The girl becomes more disobedient and blazing rows ensue. What would you do as the parent or the girl?

Who's right and who's wrong? Maybe both sides need to take a breath, count to ten and work out what's really at issue.

The issue of sex

Most of you will already know something, perhaps quite a lot, about sex. Understanding the facts is fairly straightforward. But what about the issues around sex? Is it right only to have sex when you are married? Or only with someone you love? Or only after a certain age? Attitudes to sexual **morality** have changed over the years, and they are different in different countries and cultures. You'll need to work out your own ideas about sex and what you think is right and wrong.

Love and sex

When a couple in love have sex they are enjoying more than the sexual act itself. It's a way of expressing how important they are to one another. That's why it's called 'making love'. In a loving

For many people, a loving relationship is a vital part of life.

relationship the couple respect one another as individuals who have their own thoughts and feelings, desires and ambitions. This applies to **homosexual** as well as **heterosexual** relationships.

This respect for each other means that they treat each other fairly. They only do what feels right for both partners. They care about the possible consequences of their love-making. For example, what might happen if the woman became pregnant? People are often surprised by the emotions that having sex can open up. If you're with someone who cares for you, you run less risk of getting your feelings hurt.

Marriage

In many religious traditions the view is that love and sex should be linked in marriage. It's only when you are committed to a long-term loving relationship that you should have sex. Some people believe that without marriage the link between sex and love will be broken. They believe this is wrong because sex without love is **immoral**. Many religions ask or even insist that followers respect this view.

> I think we should talk about morals in class, things like why you have sex and stuff like that… Schools just teach you the facts, and we know these already. We need to know the moral basis, otherwise all we get is the TV image and that's not how life is. On TV, boy and girl meet, have one date, go to the park, go home and have sex, which is not how it is at all. I think we need to learn how things really work between people.
>
> A 13-year-old girl quoted in *The Observer*, 27 March 1994.

SAFE SEX

Safe sex means taking precautions to protect against unwanted pregnancy and **sexually transmitted disease**. There are a number of **contraception** devices, like the Pill and condoms, to prevent women becoming pregnant when they don't want to. Condoms are also used to protect men and women against contracting a sexually transmitted disease, such as **HIV/Aids**. Most of us would agree that it is morally wrong for someone with a sexually transmittable disease not to tell whoever they are having sex with. They would be denying that person the right to know about something that could ruin their life. The other person should have the chance to decide whether they want to take the risk or to take precautions against the danger.

Many societies set legal age limits at which young people can have sex. This is the age the law considers them old enough to fully understand the possible consequences of having sex, such as pregnancy, as well as the moral issues involved.

The abortion question

Abortion – the ending of a woman's pregnancy – is an issue many people feel very strongly about. People on both sides of the debate can become very heated and emotional. For some people abortion is nothing less than the murder of an unborn child. For others, it's about a woman's **right** to choose whether she feels ready or able to cope with bringing a child into the world.

The right to life

For some people abortion is absolutely wrong and a pregnancy should never be terminated (ended). These people support the 'right to life' position, which is known as Pro-Life. Pro-lifers believe that it is wrong to kill an **embryo** or **foetus** because it is already a human being.

They say it's our duty to protect an unborn child's right to life. From their perspective, human life begins at the point of **conception**. The Pro-Lifer would also say that killing a foetus devalues human life. If you establish legally and **morally** that it's acceptable to destroy life in these cases, then all life is under threat.

Pro-Life supporters demonstrating against women's right to have abortions.

10

The right to choose

Others say it is up to the individual woman to choose whether or not she wants to give birth. This is the Pro-Choice position. Pro-Choicers argue that it's wrong to deny the woman the right to choose. They believe that an embryo or foetus is not a person yet. If it is not a person then it doesn't have the interests and rights of a person. Therefore we are not violating the rights or interests of a foetus by aborting it.

Those who are on the side of Pro-Choice also point out that if abortions became illegal, women would use so-called back-street abortionists – people who perform illegal abortions for money, often in dangerous conditions.

WHAT YOU CAN DO

- Read what you can to make yourself more aware of the issues at stake in this debate.

- If you support a particular view, you should decide whether you feel strongly enough to be actively involved in supporting it – by joining public campaigns, handing out leaflets, attending meetings and debating the issues with opponents. However, you should avoid getting involved in intimidating other people who oppose your views or who are doing their jobs.

CHANGING LAWS

Abortions were widely used as a form of **contraception** in Poland when the Communist party ruled the country. More than 100,000 abortions were carried out every year. After the fall of **Communism** in 1993 this ended. The Roman Catholic Church, which had lost its power under Communism, regained its control. It now had a powerful voice again in the affairs of the Polish people. Under pressure from the Church, which opposes abortion, the Polish parliament banned the practice in 1993. The following year there were only 786 legal abortions in the entire country.

A woman's right to choose – and a child's right to be loved and wanted?

Euthanasia — the big debate

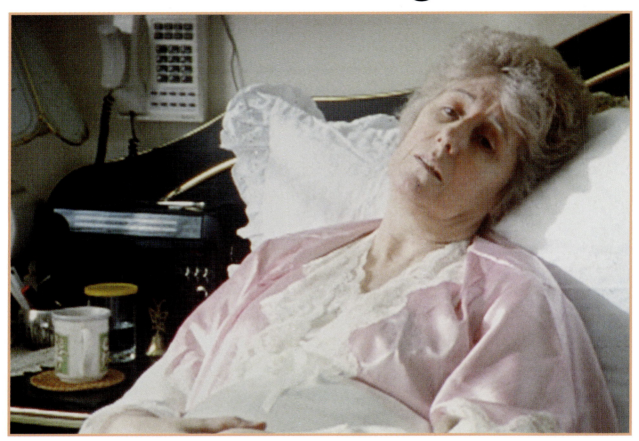

Euthanasia is the practice of helping a person who is dying in extreme pain to die more quickly, or helping a person to die who is permanently incapacitated and without hope of recovery. The purpose is to bring a person's life to an end peacefully, sparing them further pain or suffering. Although the motive may be understandable, can it ever be right to take someone's life?

A natural death

Many people are opposed to euthanasia. They feel that it is **morally** wrong, however good the intentions might be.

Terminally ill cancer patient June Burns appeared in an Australian TV advert pleading for the right to die. The advert was made for the Voluntary Euthanasia Society and increased Australia's already heated euthanasia debates.

For many religions human life is sacred and it is considered a sin to 'play God' and take someone's life. Not even extreme suffering and certain death justify it. All human life should be lived to its natural end, so there should be no interference with this process.

Those against euthanasia also argue that it's almost impossible to make strict guidelines about when it can be used. In Holland, where euthanasia is tolerated, there have been several cases for concern – including a doctor who arranged for another doctor to kill his brain-damaged son. There is also the danger, critics say, that relatives might hurry people's deaths for questionable reasons.

The right to die

However, there are many people who are in favour of euthanasia because it ends someone's suffering. They say that it's up to the individual (or their closest relatives) to decide whether they should die sooner or later. They have a **right** to choose between a lingering painful death or an early less painful one. They say that it is wrong to deny people the right to a dignified death. Some also point out that the patients would have died naturally long ago if it weren't for the drugs or medical treatment they were given, and that it's really a case of the drugs keeping them alive in an unnatural way.

The doctor's dilemma

Many doctors are against euthanasia because it is their duty to preserve human life. But at the same time they are committed to ending a person's suffering. Some doctors solve the **dilemma** by treating a patient in a way that will end in that patient's death but without actually intending to kill them. The patient is injected with a dose of painkiller to ease the pain, but large enough to also kill them. It is argued that as long as the doctor's intention was to ease the pain and not kill the patient, he or she cannot be held responsible for their death.

Dr Jack Kevorkian (centre), the euthanasia crusader branded 'Dr Death'.

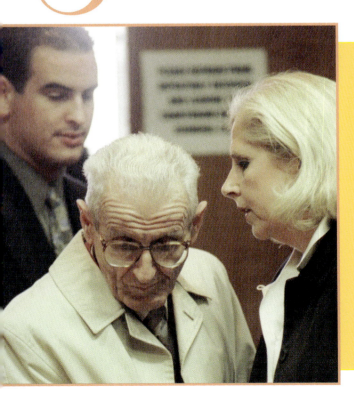

'DR DEATH'

Over ten years an American doctor, Jack Kevorkian, helped more than 130 people to commit euthanasia. The media dubbed him 'Dr Death'. He had made a 'suicide' machine with syringes containing lethal doses of drugs. He showed dying patients how they could give these drugs to themselves. Dr Kevorkian was charged and tried, but he was never found guilty of a crime. However, in March 1999, he was found guilty of murdering another terminally ill patient, Thomas Youk. This time euthanasia **campaigner** Kevorkian had injected the dose himself, and had the event filmed for a TV debate about euthanasia.

Discrimination

We can't be expected to like everybody. There are bound to be people at school, work, clubs etc, who you don't get on with. But what about people who treat others differently just because of their sex, religion, skin colour, age or other trait? Verbal or physical abuse, stereotyping and denial of basic human rights can be indications of **discrimination** or **prejudice**. Why do people discriminate against certain groups of people, and is discrimination right or wrong?

Justifying prejudice

People who are prejudiced usually give a reason. Employers who discriminate against older people say they do so because older people are not as quick as younger people. That's why they turn down older people for a job they may be fully qualified for. People who discriminate against black people might say they are responsible for more crime than white people or that they don't 'belong'. Women and girls are sometimes denied the same chances as men and boys simply because they are female. For example, women are sometimes passed over when it comes to promotion at work because employers think that if and when they have children, they will not be so committed to their work. There are laws designed to stop these kinds of discrimination, but many people still feel they are justified to think and behave as they do.

What's wrong with discrimination?

Others say that to condemn a whole group of people is wrong. It doesn't make

Many black footballers have to put up with abuse from so-called supporters.

any sense to hate all black people or to discriminate against all women. They say that treating people unfairly because you do not like them as a group is to violate their **right** to be respected as individuals. Everyone has the right to be treated equally. It's not just **morally** wrong to treat people differently, in most cases it's also legally wrong to interfere with another person's rights. Employers and individuals can be taken to court and punished for acts of discrimination.

They also say that marking out different groups is dangerous. Many black and Asian people are attacked every year as a result of prejudice. Even name-calling and minor bullying are part of the same spiral of discrimination that can lead to violence.

FOOTBALLERS AGAINST RACISM

If you've ever watched a football match, from the telly or the terraces, you'll have heard black players being abused by members of the crowd. Now footballers and others are **campaigning** to stop **racism** on the football terraces, and perhaps in other parts of society. One of the campaigns is called 'Let's Kick Racism out of Football', another is the 'Show Racism the Red Card', a European anti-racist campaign.

FACT

- *The **United Nations** has estimated that it will take until 2490 before women reach equality with men in decision-making positions.*

WHAT YOU CAN DO

If you are discriminated against you could:

- Try to sort it out first by talking to your teacher or getting advice from a Citizen's Advice Bureau.

- Get together as much evidence as you can, including statements from people who have seen what's happened.

If you see discrimination in action you could:

- Seek advice on what to do – perhaps discuss it with your parents or report it to your teacher.

- Try to persuade those who are doing it to stop.

- Make an effort to help the person being discriminated against by inviting them to join in things you are doing.

In spite of difficulties, many women are working their way up into positions of power or into jobs which would once have been thought unsuitable.

The right to privacy

In **Hitler**'s Germany in the 1930s children and adults were encouraged to spy on other people's private lives to find out who supported his rule and who didn't.

The right to invade privacy

You are free to have your privacy as long as you don't break the law or cause other people harm. If you do break the law you may face losing some of your privacy, and this would be **morally** justified. Once we commit an offence we lose the right to withhold certain information about ourselves that may be relevant to the case against us. It is an offence to lie about our private lives in order to avoid punishment for a crime. However, investigators have no right to pry into those parts of a suspect's private life that are not relevant to a case.

There are probably certain things about yourself that you do not want anyone to know, or that you only want a few people to know. You may tell these things to your family or to your closest friend, or to someone who can give you professional advice, such as your doctor. However, you only tell these people because you trust them not to tell anyone else. These things about yourself are your private concern and you have the **right** to decide who to tell about them.

Privacy and the press

The press is often criticized for invading people's privacy. Their explanation is that they are just doing their job. Many say that if people want the benefits of being famous, they should also understand that people want to know what's going on in their personal lives.

Imagine the following situation – a single man has a love affair with a famous woman who is married with two children. Journalists from the tabloid press hear of it and offer him a huge sum of money to tell the story. He knows the woman would never agree to the affair being splashed all over the newspapers and the TV, but the money is a great temptation. He tells his story. Do you think he had the right to do so? As the woman was famous, didn't the public have the right to know what was going on? What about the anguish caused to her husband and children? Or should she have thought about that before having the affair in the first place? Was the newspaper editor in the wrong for paying for the story, or was she just doing her job? What do you think?

Problems of privacy

We all hope that the people we confide in will respect our trust. Likewise, most of us try to keep the confidences of our friends or families. But what happens when there are special reasons for not doing so, like when someone tells you about something they have done wrong. What if a friend tells you he cheated in his exams? You are pretty sure that he will be found out and punished. What do you do? Are you morally obliged to tell his teacher? But that would mean breaking your friend's confidence and probably losing his friendship. He may also suffer some form of punishment, such as being expelled from the school. You could talk to him and try and persuade him to admit to what he has done. If he confesses he may get off lightly, even get a second chance. If you fail to persuade your friend to do the right thing, should you talk to someone else who may have a stronger influence over him? What would you do in this situation?

Major James Hewitt faced a barrage of criticism after he revealed to newspapers that he had an affair with Diana, Princess of Wales.

The question of lying

Be honest – how often have you told lies? Maybe they were harmless 'little white lies' to avoid getting into trouble for handing homework in late, or to make a friend feel better when he asks if his new haircut looks good. Most of us tell lies like this at some time in our lives. Yet most of us also believe that truth and honesty are important in all aspects of our lives. So is lying ever acceptable? When are lies **morally** wrong?

Do you think it's better to tell people the truth, however painful that truth might be? What if a patient is dying? Should doctors give them the facts? Do they have the right to know the truth so they can choose how to spend their remaining days?

When it's right to lie

Sometimes people lie out of a sense of duty to protect others from the harmful consequences of telling the truth. For example, a military commander when asked by journalists whether he planned to attack the enemy from a particular direction would almost certainly say he had no intention of doing that. This may in fact be his intention, but he would be putting the lives of his troops and the success of his campaign at risk if he told the media, and therefore the enemy, what he was intending to do. In this case the commander has a stronger moral duty to protect his troops than to tell the truth.

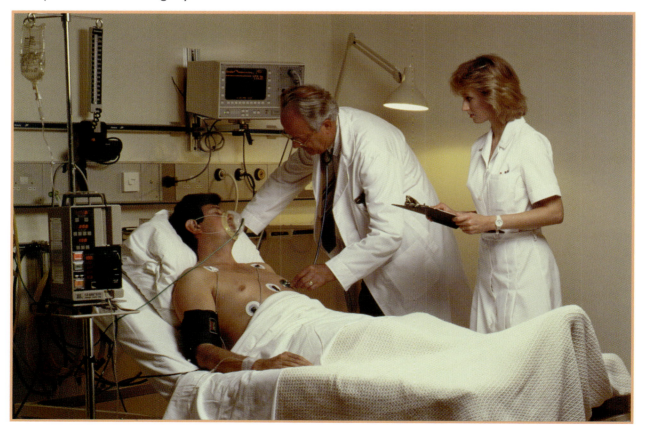

The dangers of lying

Many of us think that those 'little white lies' are acceptable. But others think that if people get away with telling small lies, it won't be long before they are telling bigger and bigger lies. Whenever possible, it is better not to tell any lies because it's difficult to draw a line between lies that are acceptable and lies that aren't.

Lying often causes more problems than it solves. You may start off telling a minor lie, but get caught up in telling more lies to keep up the story of your first lie. You may lie about who brought you home from a party. But then your dad finds out. So you tell another lie to cover up the first, and rope in a friend to back you up. Telling lies like this may get you out of trouble once or twice, but you're in danger of losing something much more important – trust. Perhaps your friend will think you might lie to her too. Or your dad will become stricter because he doesn't trust you anymore. Trust is a vital part of all our relationships and lying always puts trust at risk.

CAUGHT IN THE ACT

The political career of former British politician Jonathan Aitken was in ruins after he was caught lying in a court case. He brought the case against *The Guardian* newspaper and a TV company over their claims that a Middle Eastern businessman paid for him to spend a weekend at The Ritz Hotel in Paris. The court case was his attempt to cover up his offences, and to damage the media organizations that had uncovered his lies. Mr Aitken was later charged and tried, and he admitted his guilt and was sentenced to prison.

Former British Conservative minister Jonathan Aitken, who admitted lying to a court.

Blowing the whistle

Grigory Pasko, the Russian naval officer who became a journalist and told the world about his country's illegal dumping of nuclear waste. Nuclear waste was loaded onto ships like this one to be dumped at sea.

In 1997 Grigory Pasko, a former Russian naval officer, 'blew the whistle' on the Russian navy. The navy had been dumping nuclear waste into the Pacific Ocean around the coast of Japan. Pasko told his story to a Japanese television company who broadcast it. He was arrested and tried by a military court. The navy was not happy that Pasko had revealed their illegal activities.

Whistleblowers are people who believe they have a **moral** duty to let others know when something is being done that is illegal, unfair, or harmful to others. They believe that it's in an individual's or the public's interest that such actions are revealed and hopefully stopped. It may take great courage to speak out.

Keeping quiet

Companies sometimes expect their workers to keep all their secrets, even if the company has done something that is morally or legally wrong. If workers think something is wrong they should inform their employer, then it's up to company bosses to decide whether or not to take action. Others say it's up to the individual to take responsibility to correct a wrong they know about.

Some people believe that we aren't morally obliged to blow the whistle if it means losing our job. Although if it's a choice between saving your job and saving lives, the moral obligation is clearly to save people's lives. But what if revealing the truth about something put you and your family at risk? Would anyone blame you for putting your family's lives first?

The case for telling

Engineers at the Ford motor company in the USA discovered that the petrol tanks of the company's Pinto model were likely to explode if another car crashed into the back of it. When told, the company's executives chose to keep quiet and not recall the vehicles with the dangerous tanks. This was a violation of people's **rights**. Pinto car owners had a right to know what was going on – they had a right to know their lives were in danger. The engineers finally revealed the truth because they felt a duty to tell people about the risks of buying a Pinto car or continuing to drive the one they had.

THINK IT OVER

If you knew that an older boy in your school was bullying a younger boy, what would you do about it? Would you want to put a stop to it and if so how? Would you tell your teacher what was going on? If you did you would be 'blowing the whistle' on the bully. In doing this you would be taking a moral stand against bullying.

THE *CHALLENGER* TRAGEDY

On 28 January 1986 the space shuttle *Challenger* blasted off from NASA's (National Aeronautics and Space Administration) launch pad in Florida, USA. On board were seven crew members, including a schoolteacher, Christa McAuliffe, who planned to give lessons from space. What the public didn't know was that the shuttle's engineers had warned NASA about a design fault in its booster rockets. NASA managers went ahead with the launch despite these warnings. Seventy-three seconds after blast-off the shuttle exploded, killing all on board. The world was outraged to hear the tragedy could have been averted, when engineers told of the booster problems and the warnings they had given the managers.

There was a stunned silence at Cape Canaveral launch site as *Challenger* exploded into a fireball.

The drug problem

Today stories about the effects and problems associated with **illegal drugs** are commonplace. Almost everyone knows that some drugs affect people's actions and judgement so they take harmful or fatal risks. Horror stories abound of young people who have died instantly after reacting badly to a drug they took for fun, or of others who have died by choking on their own vomit. But would these things happen less often if drugs like heroin were **legalized**? Some people think this would help solve the problem. Others do not.

For legalizing drugs

Some people think we should be allowed to choose what we do in our free time. After all, we know that tobacco and alcohol cause damage, but apart from an age limit there is no ban on their use. There is also the fact that while many drugs are illegal, it hasn't stopped people buying and using them, so what's the point? Prohibiting certain drugs just makes them more glamorous. It also means that criminals benefit by being able to sell them at high prices.

Even if there were more drug-users after legalization, the advantages would outweigh the disadvantages. Drugs would become cheaper and easier to buy, which would mean there would be less need for people to get involved in crime and take other desperate measures to get the money to buy them. The vast

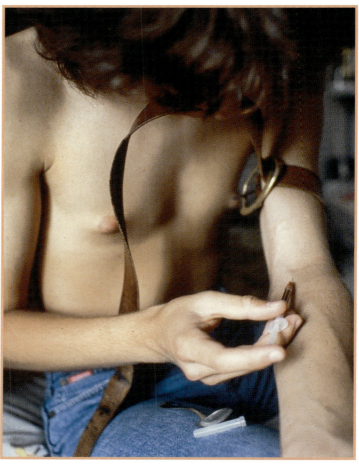

Injecting is the riskiest way of getting drugs into the body. Dirty needles spread infections and cause other problems, such as blood poisoning. If one limb is injected too much, problems may occur which mean the limb must be amputated.

amounts of money used in policing drug-related crime could then be used for other police work.

Against legalizing drugs

Those against legalizing drugs say it would be disastrous. We already know that the use of certain drugs harms people. So, giving people the right to use

FACTS

● An increasing number of road accidents are caused by drivers under the influence of drugs.

● About 15 per cent of the people who seek help for drug problems at UK agencies are under 20 years old.

Taking drugs causes problems. Young people involved with drugs may lose their place at school or college, lose friends or be thrown out by their families. They run out of money and may steal to feed their habit.

those drugs is **morally** wrong. People who become hooked on drugs may destroy their health, ruin their education or careers, hurt their children and partners, cause fatal car accidents, and kill themselves through overdosing. If drugs were more readily available, more people would take them and these terrible problems would only increase.

They say that to claim people should have the **right** to choose is not good enough. It's not just the business of the individual. The use of drugs is other people's business because it causes people to behave in ways that affect and sometimes hurt other people.

WHAT YOU CAN DO

● If drugs are being used or sold in your school, consider reporting it to your teacher or head teacher. You may want to talk to someone close to you before you decide what to do, perhaps your parents.

● Avoid getting involved with anyone who is close to the drug scene.

● Inform yourself. Think carefully about where you stand on this issue.

The aims of punishment

This picture shows a prison officer at the command post of a high-security prison in Arizona, USA. This special unit holds 114 out of the state's total 119 inmates who have been condemned to death.

You know there are rules at your school that you have to follow and that if you get caught breaking them you could be punished. The same goes for a footballer who is caught breaking the rules of the game. This also applies to those caught breaking the laws of the land. How they are punished depends on how serious the offence is. But what is the point of such punishment, and does it achieve what it sets out to do? One of the biggest debates around punishment is whether **capital punishment** is ever **morally** acceptable.

What's the point?

People have different views about the aims of punishment. Some say that punishment is simply a way of making the offender pay for their offence. There is no other point to it. This is based on the 'eye for an eye' or **retribution** principle. The idea is that the punishment should match the crime. For example, if someone kills another person, they should pay for that crime with their own life.

Others say that the aim of punishment is to deter (put off) people from breaking rules or laws again. It is hoped that the offender will dislike losing their freedom so much that it will ensure they don't commit crimes again. It also serves to warn others that if they break the law they too will be punished. This is the **deterrence** idea of punishment.

Another possible aim of punishment is to **reform** (change) the individual. The aim is to improve the moral outlook of the individual while they're in prison so that when they leave they know the right way to behave. To this end, prisoners are offered education and training to give them different options for the future.

Should we kill killers?

The most severe punishment that any society can inflict on an offender is death. This is known as capital punishment. Where it is still practised in the Western world, such as in parts of the USA, it applies to those who commit murder, treason (betraying your government or country) and certain military offences.

What are the rights and wrongs of capital punishment? Some say there is no clear evidence that capital punishment is any better a deterrent than a long prison sentence. They say that there are no benefits – **executing** someone only adds to the amount of misery in the world. They say that if murder is wrong, then how can execution ever be acceptable? There have been instances in which innocent people have been executed. If they had been serving a prison sentence, they could have been released and given the chance to live the rest of their life in freedom.

> ### FACTS
>
> - *Britain is one of 69 countries which no longer has the death penalty for any crime; another 13 only use it for particular crimes such as treason; and 23 have not used it for ten years or more.*
> - *In 1998, 1067 known executions were carried out in the world – it is believed that the actual figure was far higher.*

A case for reform? Jimmy Boyle, a convicted killer from Glasgow, Scotland, became an artist during his spell in prison. He is a reformed character and his work is now taken seriously by art critics.

25

The rights and wrongs of aid

Very little touches us more than the sight of children dying of starvation or the despair of people living on the street. In the face of suffering many of us will do something to help, perhaps by donating money to the agencies or charities that give aid to people in need. Others say that it isn't their business – that it's the responsibility of governments to do something. Should you help all you can or should you leave it to others? And what if you do nothing? Should you worry about that?

Is it wrong to do nothing?

Surely we cannot criticize someone for doing nothing? Why should people give away their hard-earned cash to help others? If we are relatively well-off we've got the right to keep our money, even if other people are starving to death. Why should we feel guilty if we choose to spend it in other ways?

Yet others say that we have a **moral** responsibility to help others if we can. If people suffer from hunger or disease, or even die and we stand by doing nothing, we are guilty of letting them suffer. It doesn't matter how far away those people might be, or that we may never meet them, there are consequences to our actions – and doing nothing to help is as much a decisive action as doing something to help.

Victims of famine wait in line for food during Somalia's civil war.

Oxfam development workers and local villagers sink a water well for a Cambodian community.

Why bother?

Many people who do not give to charities or aid agencies say it's because the small amount they could give wouldn't make any difference. Or that they can't be sure the money they give will all be used for good causes, and that some of it may be wasted by organizers or governments.

Yet charities themselves insist that every little helps, and that if everybody gave donations, however small, they would be able to offer help and hope to millions of people across the world. Surely it's worth giving up some of our money to help the suffering of others? Charities only ask us to give whatever we can, not amounts that would mean we had to neglect ourselves.

CANCELLING DEBT

The US President, Bill Clinton, announced at the end of September 1999 that America would cancel all debts owed to it by poorer nations. The President said that America had a 'moral imperative' to help those countries whose progress was being seriously hampered by debts to the richer countries. He was responding to the growing **campaign** by religious leaders and others for the cancellation of these debts. In December 1999 the British government announced that it was cancelling all debt owed to it by the **developing world**.

WHAT YOU CAN DO

- Give money to the international charities that help people in need, like Oxfam, Save the Children or Christian Aid. Or ring them and find out how you can help.

- Make a difference just by buying **fair-trade** goods from charity shops or supermarkets.

FACTS

- *One-fifth of the world's population lives in absolute poverty.*
- *Almost 800 million people do not get enough food, and 500 million are severely underfed.*
- *In the developing world 1.3 billion people lack drinking water and 2.9 billion do not have safe sanitation (drainage and sewage).*

I have seen repeatedly on my travels what a vital contribution the British aid programme makes in developing countries. In countries like Sudan it means the difference between life and death for thousands.

George Carey, Archbishop of Canterbury, England, 1996

Morals at work

Some **professional** people behave in ways that would not be tolerated in normal life. It is fully expected, for example, that lawyers will lie and soldiers may kill. We allow this because certain professions need different **moral** codes to be able to do their jobs properly. But is it really necessary or acceptable for some professions to behave in ways that we would usually condemn?

A lawyer speaks to the jury in a courtroom. It's up to the jury to decide whether she and her client are telling the truth.

THE LAWYER

Consider the case of a lawyer whose client is pleading 'not guilty' to murder. She has a duty to defend her client as best she can, even if she suspects he is guilty. The client tells her that one of the witnesses may give evidence that will prove his guilt. To prevent this, the lawyer discredits the witness's evidence when she questions him in court.

Normally, we would consider it morally wrong to interfere with such evidence. However, the lawyer is defending her client's **rights**. The 'not guilty' plea commits the lawyer, legally and morally, to defend her client as if he were innocent, whatever she may think. The lawyer is obliged by law to keep secret what she knows about her client's guilt.

THE SOLDIER

For soldiers to be able to do their difficult job, they have a different set of moral rules. These are not personal or private codes of behaviour, they only apply when the individuals are acting as soldiers. The rules of combat mean that soldiers are protected from personal and moral blame if they kill someone in combat. They also follow rules about the fair treatment of prisoners of war and **civilians**.

However, there have been times when soldiers break their own rules. During the **Vietnam War**, some American soldiers committed serious offences that crossed over the bounds of what they were entitled to do as soldiers. They killed innocent civilians, a crime for which some of them were later tried in court.

THE BUSINESS PERSON

Many business people claim that lying or bluffing to get the best deals is part of the moral code for doing business, and that if you didn't do it you wouldn't be looking after your best interests – making money. As long as you don't break the laws of the land, they say, what you do is morally acceptable. These 'rules' allow you to deceive others, conceal the truth about a product, and overcharge customers, among other things.

But can people in business really set themselves outside the normal moral codes? When the consequences of lying aren't important it might not matter. But if the consequences are serious, as when manufacturers target cigarette sales at very young people, it does matter. Surely it's no excuse to say that if one business doesn't do it, others will?

TOBACCO GIANT SCANDAL

In February 2000 the world's second largest international cigarette company, British American Tobacco (BAT), was accused of smuggling on a world scale. BAT bosses arranged to supply vast numbers of cigarettes to certain distributors knowing they would find their way onto the '**black market**'. Cigarettes sold like this are cheaper and are often sold illegally to children and young people. This helps to lure generations of new smokers.

US soldiers wait in a bunker before carrying out an assault during the Vietnam war.

The right to protest

Imagine you hear about plans to build a bypass round the small town where you live. You are against the new road because it means destroying an important local wildlife area. So you join a local protest group and take part in public protests to show how you feel. In many countries across the world people have the **right** to protest like this, as long as they do so peacefully. Only if protests become disruptive should the police stop them. Yet sometimes ordinary people take part in illegal protests because they feel that their cause is more important than their duty to obey the law. Are they right? Or are there other, equally effective ways of taking action?

Kids for Clean Water march across the beach for the Heal the Bay demonstration, campaigning for a clean environment in Los Angeles, California in June 1989.

A duty to break the law

Some say we have a duty to break the law if it means that we draw more attention to an injustice that needs to be corrected. They would have agreed with the people of Bridlington, Essex, UK, who, in 1998, blocked a public road to stop trucks carrying live calves. The animals were on their way to Spain where they were to be slaughtered for meat. People were protesting about the conditions in which the animals were being kept on a long journey. They also hoped to force animal transport companies to improve the conditions of transport for the animals. Most of the people involved were ordinary, law-abiding folk, but they faced a conflict of interests. While they would have preferred not to break the law, they felt that protesting against cruelty to young animals was more important.

Extremism and protest

Sometimes even when people try to protest peacefully, things go wrong. In June 1999 there was a peaceful 'fun protest' in London's financial district against Developing World debt, the arms trade and the greed of big companies. Unfortunately, the peaceful demonstrators had their protest hijacked by a group of **extremists**. The protest turned violent when extremists fought the police and rampaged through the streets damaging property and injuring people. The rights of the majority to protest peacefully were ruined, and many said that the actions of the extremists had damaged, not helped, their cause. Instead of reporting on the worthwhile causes of the protest, newspapers and TV programmes highlighted the violence instead.

People are entitled to protest peacefully, but sometimes police step in when they think things are getting out of hand.

WHAT YOU CAN DO

- If you want to take action to change something, you could join an organization involved in trying to put things right. If you do, make sure you know as much as possible about the issue you are protesting about.

- Always respect the rights of innocent people, even those opposed to what you stand for. This is a free society in which everyone is entitled to express his or her opinion. If they are doing no more than that, there is no justification for interfering.

Tampering with nature

Scientific progress in the 21st century is leading us onto tricky **moral** ground. Many new developments raise difficult questions about the moral rights and wrongs of using them. Is it right to tamper with nature just because scientific research has made it possible? How do you feel about research being carried out on human **embryos**? Should scientists be experimenting with **genes**? How far should we let science go?

Experimenting on human embryos

Many medical advances have been made through experimenting on embryos taken from abortions. For many people this is morally wrong. To them an embryo is a potential human life, which is sacred. They say that to kill embryos is to devalue all human life.

Dolly is probably the most famous sheep in the world. She is a **clone** – she has exactly the same genes as her parents and was created in the laboratory by scientists.

On the other hand some people accept the experiments because they do not think that embryos are fully formed human beings. Also, they believe that such research is justified because it helps scientists find new ways to combat disease.

Gene research

There are several different kinds of research using genes. Research is being done with human genes to develop new medical treatments, and with plant genes to improve crops. There is also research into using genes to replicate (copy) animal strains or types.

Gene research raises serious moral problems. Many people object to scientists changing natural things artificially. Many are not even convinced that the results are worthwhile. They are particularly worried by the practice of taking genes from one animal and developing a similar type animal with the same characteristics, as in the clone 'Dolly' the sheep. The fear is that we may move on to cloning human beings in the same way.

Surrogate mothers

A woman who is unable to have a child naturally because she or her partner is **infertile** may use a medical technique called *in-vitro* **fertilization (IVF)** to have a baby. If a woman is unable to carry a baby through the period of pregnancy for health reasons, the fertilized egg can be placed in another woman's body. The other woman becomes the 'surrogate' mother.

For some people, babies should only be brought into the world naturally, and within marriage, and so they are against the idea of surrogate mothers. Some people have also accused surrogate mothers of selling babies because they have been paid to carry a child for another woman. But there are others who say that without IVF many couples who long to be parents, and who would make very good parents, would never be able to have children of their own.

FRANKENSTEIN FOODS?

GM (genetically modified) crops are plants that have had their genes altered to make them capable of giving greater yields, resisting disease or even drought (lack of water). Many people feel that these plants should not be grown without proper testing, when no-one really knows what effects growing and eating them could have on the environment or on our health. Many individuals are refusing to buy GM foods and environmental groups are campaigning for a ban on GM foods for five years, when there will have been time to test them fully.

GM crops – food miracle or menace?

People before profit?

You may find it hard to understand how a company can announce multi-million dollar profits one day and sack thousands of workers the next in order to increase its future profits. Shouldn't companies have a sense of **moral** or social responsibility for their workers and for the society that has to support those left unemployed? Why should the **shareholders** be satisfied at the expense of other people?

Business responsibilities

Many business people say that a company's only responsibility is to make as much profit as it can for its shareholders. They also say that business people cannot and should not get involved in making decisions and taking actions to improve people's welfare, the environment or whatever else. Businesses are private enterprises and should not meddle in public affairs. Many say businesses are already doing their bit – by pursuing profit they generate the wealth needed to give the rest of us the standard of living we enjoy.

Is it the case that for many companies the profits on the chart are more important than people?

It's more than just profits

However, others say that business people are responsible for more than profits. They have responsibilities to the consumers who buy or use their products, their employees and suppliers. In fact it makes good business sense to behave in more responsible ways because today many consumers buy products on the basis of where and how they were made. For example, many people try to buy **fair-trade** goods that are made without exploiting other people.

Some companies do have morals

Companies in some countries have now recognized the importance of moral codes of conduct. In America 60 per cent of companies have some kind of moral code of behaviour for doing business at home and abroad. The codes cover the

Is pollution a necessary evil if companies are to produce the goods we need, or could they produce them in a more environmentally friendly way?

way they treat customers, employees, shareholders and suppliers. Some business schools are even running classes in **ethics**. Despite this, moral codes are often broken when they clash with the company's financial interests.

WHO CARES ABOUT THE ENVIRONMENT?

If factories are responsible for polluting the environment, should they clean it up? In some parts of the world, such as in the USA and Europe, companies are legally bound to pay for cleaning up the pollution they cause. The money for this is raised through special taxes and a 'polluter-pays' policy, which means if a company pollutes, it has to pay to clean up the damage. Companies sometimes argue that they would like to be more **environmentally friendly**, but the costs are too high. Higher costs mean that companies have to charge people more for their products. People don't want to pay more, so companies can't afford to care more for the environment. So who does care?

COMPANY MAN WITH A CONSCIENCE

In January 2000 one of the most successful businessmen in the world gave $750 million to charity. One reporter estimated that Bill Gates, owner of the hugely successful Microsoft Corporation, an international computer company, had given in one payment five times the amount the US government gave in aid in one year.

It's not my fault!

'It's not my fault, it was her idea. She told me to do it.' How much can we blame other people or organizations for our actions? When we criticize a school, hospital or company, who's really responsible? Is it the individuals who are the problem, or are they only following company policy? Even if they are following rules, is that good enough? Don't we all have to make our own decisions about what's right and wrong, instead of passing the responsibility onto others?

It is always easy to blame others for things we have done wrong but taking responsibility for our actions is the best thing to do.

Trouble at the top

We often talk about organizations as if they were **morally** responsible. We might hold them responsible for breaking the law, for ignoring safety regulations, for polluting the environment, and so on. But should it be a company or organization that is held responsible, or the people who run it? Obviously you can't imprison or punish an organization. It's the people who work for it, especially those at the top, who give the orders, who should be punished if things go wrong.

Following the rules

But what if the individuals are simply following company policy? Most organizations have to be run in a certain way, independent of the individuals who make it up. For example, say a government agreed to sell fighter jets to a foreign government on the promise they would be used for defensive purposes only. This decision was taken by people who probably realized that there was a good chance the weapons would be used against that country's own people, to stop them criticizing their leaders. To most people, this would be thought of as **immoral**. But who's to blame? After all, the decision was made in line with government policy. Would you blame the government or the individuals concerned?

The foreign secretary who signed the agreement to sell the jets would say it was a decision made by the government. The government would say they made the decision on the advice of senior government advisors, taking into account the interests of their country's people. Perhaps the other country buys certain products that would create or save jobs and refusing the jets would have jeopardized other deals. The government may even claim that the decision was based on an established policy, inherited from a previous government. What do you think?

PAID TO KILL

In January 2000, Dr Harold Shipman, a trusted family doctor, became Britain's most infamous serial killer. He was convicted of killing 15 elderly female patients and of forging a will for £386,000. But he is actually suspected of killing about 150 of his patients.

Who's to blame in a situation such as this? Is it fair to blame the organizations involved? After all, to them and to the rest of the world, Shipman appeared to be a caring family doctor. Shipman had been cunning and deceptive and had hidden his actions from those around him. In the trial Shipman was found to be entirely responsible for his crimes. The Conservative health spokesman, Dr Liam Fox, said that it was one doctor who had been found guilty 'not the medical profession and not general practitioners'.

The rights and wrongs of war

A war is being fought every day somewhere in the world. People are killing and being killed – soldiers and **civilians**. Television brings some of these wars into our living rooms so we see and hear what's going on. Most of us would say that in principle war is wrong, not least because it involves killing other human beings, and that if possible it should be avoided. However, we may have no choice but to go to war. And in wars soldiers will have no choice but to fight and kill. Or do they? Are there still **moral** choices to be made? What are the rights and wrongs of war?

At a rally in Los Angeles in January 1991, people hold up signs protesting US involvement in the war in the Persian Gulf.

Pacifism

A pacifist is someone who believes that it's wrong to kill another person and that you should never do so, no matter what. You shouldn't kill to save yourself or anyone else, not even your wife or children. Some pacifists don't hold such an extreme view. They accept there are rare occasions when war is justified. But even then you still have to justify killing another human being as vigorously as you would in peacetime, which you would normally find hard to bear. Pacifists say it shouldn't be easier to kill just because it's war.

NUCLEAR WAR

There is probably no worse prospect for the human race than **nuclear war**. How can we justify nuclear war when it involves massive loss of life and property, and maybe the destruction of the human race? Some people believe that it may be justifiable if it were contained as a small-scale conflict between two nations. Others fear that a small-scale nuclear war might lead to a wider use of nuclear weapons, which in turn might lead to a larger-scale nuclear war. With such threat to human life, perhaps we would be better off without nuclear arms altogether?

During the **Gulf War**, civilians in Baghdad, Iraq, died when a bomb shelter was bombed by mistake.

Innocent victims

Killing another human being in combat is one thing, but killing innocent civilians is another. For many this is unacceptable, and yet in modern warfare, despite and because of, high-tech weapons, such as guided missiles, it's often impossible to distinguish between civilians and military targets. In war you can only justify intentionally killing someone who is threatening your life. Civilians are not directly involved in war and should not be attacked.

However, civilians are sometimes killed unintentionally, as part of the effect of bombing or attacking military targets, such as a bridge or a weapons factory. Collateral damage is the term used to indicate unintentional harm to civilians. Military leaders say they cannot be held responsible for the damage because the intention was to destroy the military targets, not to destroy homes and kill innocent people. However, to attack a troop carrier with 50 soldiers aboard and mistakenly cause the death of 500 civilians is hard to justify.

FACTS

- *In the last ten years of the 20th century over 10 million children and young people had direct experience of the horrors of war.*
- *About 90 per cent of all the casualties in modern wars are civilians.*
- *Worldwide, about 300,000 children, some as young as seven, fight in armed conflicts every day.*

Terrorism

Terrorists use violence to try and achieve a political aim. They may want a government to change policies or release a **political prisoner**. They use terror to get people's attention and to get their cause into the news. Terrorists use various methods including bombing, shooting, **hijacking** vehicles or taking **hostages**. Many victims of terrorism are innocent civilians who have nothing to do with the terrorists' cause. So can terrorists ever justify their actions?

The terrorist position

The terrorist might say that the **assassination** of a leader who is causing great suffering is **morally** justified because the suffering would then end. For example, if **Hitler** had been assassinated in 1936 many people in Germany would not have been persecuted and ended up in concentration camps, and we might never have gone to war in 1939. So good consequences could follow from killing someone who is evil.

Some terrorists believe they are fighting a war and think of themselves as soldiers. They say that deaths are accepted in war and that is what they are fighting, even if the 'other side' refuses to call it a war.

Terrorists also say that sometimes violence is necessary to bring about change. It's the only way to make some people listen. They say that as long as the aim is to bring about a positive change, the means are justified.

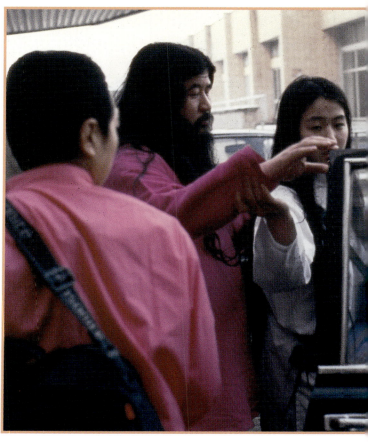

In 1995 a fanatical Japanese religious group, Aum Shinrikyo (which means 'supreme truth'), released poisonous gas on the Tokyo underground. Their blind leader, Shoko Asahara (seen here being helped into a car), often refers to the power of poison gas. It is thought that this terrorist act was aimed at government workers whose offices were nearby. Twelve people died and 5000 were injured.

The anti-terrorist position

One problem with the idea of assassinating a leader like Hitler is that there is no guarantee that by getting rid of one evil person the situation will improve. It might actually get worse. Terrorists represent a relatively small group of people, so why should they be allowed to enforce their will on other people?

Also, it is often said that in a democratic society, it should be possible to resolve political problems without the need for terrorism. If a cause is just, it should be possible to achieve the same goals through debate and by persuading people to vote in your favour. Political change should only occur if the majority of people want it to.

One of the dangers of terrorism is that violence may become an established way of trying to change society. What if people used violence to oppose everything they disagreed with? People would learn to live with violence and some might even begin to enjoy the feeling of power it gave them.

AIRPORT DANGER

Airports and planes are often the targets of terrorist attacks. That's why your luggage is searched before you can board a plane. Security is an important weapon in the fight against terrorism. Ways of finding weapons and explosives include X-ray machines, metal detectors and sniffer dogs, which are trained to find stashes of explosives.

THE BOMBING OF OKLAHOMA CITY

On 19 April 1995 a massive bomb exploded outside a public building in Oklahoma City, USA, killing nearly 200 people and injuring hundreds more. It was later discovered that this was the act of a small group of **extremists** who carried out the terrorist attack because of a grievance they had against the US government.

The value of nature

The house you live in, the school you attend, the pavements and streets you walk along, have all been built on what was originally wild countryside. Human beings have always used the environment for their own purposes, often in ways that go beyond satisfying basic needs such as shelter and food. If you live in a big city you will know how little natural space there is to enjoy and how far you have to travel to reach it. Should we continue using up nature like this, or should we try to strike some balance between what we need and what nature needs?

Are all living things equal?

Some people believe that nature only exists for humans to use in the way they want. In this view nature has no value in itself and so there is no need to respect it. It only has a value in what it can do for us – as a source of food, wealth, pleasure and so on.

Others say that nature doesn't just serve the needs of people, that it's valuable in itself. So we should respect it and use it only because we need to. We need food and therefore have to cultivate crops or rear animals on land that may have to be cleared of its natural cover. It's okay to kill animals, but only for food.

Humans or nature?

Sometimes we may have to decide whether the interests of humans are more important than saving wildlife or countryside. This **dilemma** often occurs when plans are announced for building a new road. What's more important, to ease the traffic pressure on a town or protect important wildlife habitats? It's a complicated issue. People living in a town might say they need the new road because their health is threatened by the pollution caused by the heavy traffic. They might also say that families in the town need the work that the new road might create.

Brown pelicans are an endangered species. Their population declined due to the use of pesticides.

Striking a balance

Environmentalists say we should weigh up the short-term advantages of building a bypass for example with the long-term damage that it will have on the environment. They say we have a duty to save the environment for future generations. Nature provides us with healthy air, fertile soils, clean waterways, food, open space and recreation. They say there are other ways of helping people without damaging the environment. For example, public transport could be improved, reducing the number of cars on the roads. Looking after the environment is actually the best way of looking after ourselves.

Many people believe that by wrecking the planet we are destroying our future. Is looking after the environment also the best way of looking after ourselves?

FACTS

- *Worldwide, over 1000 different species of birds and mammals are extremely rare.*
- *There are now around 500 million cars polluting the planet. Pollution is believed to cause climate change which scientists believe causes some natural disasters.*
- *Modern farming methods have caused a serious decline in bird populations.*
- *Thirteen of the world's fifteen fishing grounds are overfished or fished to the limit.*

WHAT YOU CAN DO

- Use public transport when you can, and cycle or walk whenever possible.

- Recycle and reuse whatever you can – paper, tins, bottles, etc. Encourage your school and family to recycle as well.

- Buy recycled products. Refuse to take unnecessary packaging when you buy anything. Reuse things like envelopes and bags as much as you can.

- Get your family to replace its lightbulbs with low-energy lightbulbs.

- Save water – take showers instead of baths.

- Join a local or international environment or wildlife group and help them with their **campaigns** or fund-raising. (See page 46 for addresses.)

Glossary

anorexic condition which leaves the sufferer obsessed with losing weight to the extent that they may damage their health, or in some cases die

assassination the killing of one person (usually a political leader) by another person for political reasons

black market sale of illegal or smuggled goods

campaign an organized attempt to persuade others to change something

capital punishment the execution of someone for crimes such as murder and treason

civilians people not directly involved in fighting a war

clone living thing created by replicating (copying) the genes of a parent. The genetic make-up of a clone is identical to that of its parent.

Communism political system in which all property is publicly owned and each person is paid and works according to his or her own needs and abilities

conception the point at which a male sperm joins with a female egg and a baby starts to develop

consumers people who buy products that are for sale

contraception measures taken to prevent pregnancy

deterrence the idea that punishing people who have committed an offence, or might commit one, may put them off doing it in the future

developing world poorer countries that are trying to develop their economies to catch up with the richer countries of the world

dilemma situation in which you have to choose between two equally desirable or undesirable alternatives

discrimination treating people unfairly because of their race, gender, nationality or ethnic background

embryo term used for an unborn child up to the end of the first eight weeks of its life. After that it is called a foetus.

environmentalist someone who pursues an interest in saving and protecting the environment from damage

environmentally friendly behaving in a way which does not harm the environment, but instead maintains or nurtures it

ethics moral principles

execution the official killing of someone who has committed a crime. The methods used include firing squad, hanging, beheading, gassing, electrocution, lethal injection.

extremists people who hold extreme or fanatical religious or political views

fair trade producers of fair-trade goods have all been paid fair wages, work in good conditions and are treated fairly

foetus the term used for an unborn child after the age of eight weeks

genes the material in your body that makes you a unique individual

GM (genetically modified) food grown from crop seeds that have been artificially changed in the laboratory to make crops more resistant to disease or to make them produce higher yields

Gulf War war between Iraq in the Middle East and 23 nations led by the USA

heterosexual physically and emotionally attracted to members of the opposite sex

hijacking when a lorry, plane or other vehicle is taken over and forced to go to a different destination

Hitler, Adolf leader of the Nazi Party in Germany, the political group in the 1930s and early 1940s that started World War II in 1939

HIV/Aids HIV is a virus which attacks the white blood cells that protect the body from disease. People with HIV eventually become ill and are said to have AIDS (Acquired Immune Deficiency Syndrome).

homosexual physically and emotionally attracted to members of the same sex

hostages people taken prisoner and held until their jailers' demands are met

illegal drugs drugs controlled by laws that state who can use and supply them. Some are for medicinal use by doctors permission only.

immoral a term used to describe behaviour that goes against what is generally regarded by a community as good and right

infertile physically unable to produce children

in-vitro fertilization (IVF) method of helping an infertile woman to become pregnant. This involves fertilizing the woman's egg with the man's sperm in a laboratory. The egg is then placed in the woman's body (in the ovum) so that she becomes pregnant.

legalized allowed by law. In the case of drugs it means they could be used without restrictions.

moral a term used to describe behaviour that is generally regarded by a community as good and right

nuclear war war that involves the use of nuclear weapons

political prisoners people imprisoned for their political views, not for a criminal act

prejudice treating someone differently because of a biased view you hold about their race, religion, sex etc.

professionals people who do certain jobs, such as lawyers, doctors, teachers, that require qualifications and are controlled by certain rules and regulations

racism the belief that people of certain races are inferior or superior

reform change the attitude of people to make them behave better

refugees people who have left their own home or country because of war or another situation that makes it dangerous for them to stay

retribution the idea of punishing someone simply because they have committed an offence and deserve to be punished – there is no other purpose to punishment in this view

rights things to which you are morally and socially and sometimes legally entitled, such as fair treatment

sexually transmitted disease disease passed on during sexual intercourse

shareholders people who take a share in a company by investing money in it

terminally ill suffering an illness or disease which will inevitably lead to death

taxes money paid to governments by citizens to pay for the needs of a country, such as roads, education, armies and health services

transplant to replace an unhealthy organ (such as a heart) in the human body with a healthy one

United Nations international organization to maintain peace and security throughout the world. The UN also has specialized agencies dealing with things like health, education and discrimination.

Vietnam War American war against Communist North Vietnam from 1964–75

Contacts and helplines

AMNESTY INTERNATIONAL
99–119 Rosebery Avenue
London, EC1R 4RE
020 7814 6200

CAMPAIGN FOR NUCLEAR DISARMAMENT
162 Holloway Road, London, N7 8DQ
020 7700 2393
www.cnduk.org/welcome.htm

CHRISTIAN AID
PO Box 100
London, SE1 7RT
020 7620 4444
www.christian-aid.org.uk

COMMISSION FOR RACIAL EQUALITY
Elliot House , 10–12 Allington Street
London, SW1E 5EH
020 7828 7022

ENVIRONMENT AGENCY
0845 933 3111
(to find the contact details for your local office)

EQUAL OPPORTUNITIES COMMISSION
Customer Contact Point, Overseas House
Quay Street, Manchester, M3 3HN
0161 833 9244
www.eoc.org.uk

GREENPEACE
Canonbury Villas, London, N1 2PN
020 7865 8100

ISDD (INSTITUTE FOR THE STUDY OF DRUG DEPENDENCE)
Waterbridge House, 32–36 Loman Street
London SE1 0EE
020 7928 1211

NATIONAL ABORTION CAMPAIGN
18 Ashwin Street
London, E8 3PL

OXFAM
274 Banbury Road
Oxford, OX2 7DZ

REFUGEE COUNCIL
3 Bondway, London, SW8 1SJ
020 7820 3000

THE VOLUNTARY EUTHANASIA SOCIETY
13 Prince of Wales Terrace
London, W8 5PG
020 7937 7770
dialspace.dial.pipex.com/ves.london

WOMANKIND WORLDWIDE
3 Albion Place
London, W6 0LT
020 8563 8607/8

WORLDWIDE FUND FOR NATURE
11–13 Ockford Road
Godalming
Surrey, GU7 1QU

IN AUSTRALIA

AMNESTY INTERNATIONAL AUSTRALIA
National Office, National Private Bag 23
Broadway, NSW 2007
02 9217 7600

HUMAN RIGHTS AND EQUAL OPPORTUNITIES COMMISSION
Level 8, Piccadilly Tower
133 Castlereagh Street
Sydney, NSW 2000
02 9284 9600

Further reading

Non-fiction

Free publication from the Commission for Racial Equality:
Rights and Responsibilities Pack, including A2 posters, postcards and A5 leaflets with information about the laws against racial discrimination and harassment, and what can be done to combat racism

Books

Contemporary Moral Issues
Joe Jenkins, Heinemann 1997

Roots of the Future: ethnic diversity in the making of Britain
CRE Publications
Also available are posters from the book, including: Henry VIII's trumpeters; Olaudah Equiano; Isambard Kingdom Brunel; Benjamin Disraeli.

Video

Show Racism the Red Card
This comes with study notes and an educational magazine.
www.srtrc.org

Index

abortion 4, 10-11, 32
absolute principles 4
Aitken, Jonathan 19
animal exports 30
anorexia 5
assassinations 40
Aum Shinrikyo 40
black market 29
blaming others 4, 36, 37
Boyle, Jimmy 25
British American Tobacco (BAT) 29
bullying 14, 21
business
    company policies 37
    moral codes and responsibilities 29, 34-5, 36
    whistleblowers 20-1
capital punishment 24, 25
Challenger space shuttle 21
charities/aid agencies 26-27
cheating 17
child soldiers 39
children's rights 6
civilian casualties 28, 38-9, 40
climate change 43
cloning 32, 33
confidences, keeping 5, 16
contraception 9, 11
crime 5, 16, 24-5
developing world debt cancellation 27
Diana, Princess of Wales 17
dilemmas 4-5, 7, 13, 42
discrimination 14-15
drugs 22-3
embryo research 32
energy conservation 43
environmental issues 30, 35, 42-3
ethics 35
euthanasia 4, 5, 12-13
extremism 31, 41
fair-trade goods 27, 35

family relationships 6-7
famine and poverty 26-7
Ford motor company 21
freedom of opinion 31
Gates, Bill 35
gene research 32-3
GM (genetically modified) crops 33
grounding 7
Gulf War 38, 39
Hewitt, Major James 17
hijacking 40
Hitler, Adolf 40
HIV/Aids 9
homosexuality 8
hostage-taking 40
human rights 14
in-vitro fertilization (IVF) 33
infertility 33
Kevorkian, Dr Jack 13
killing in combat 4, 28, 38
legal profession 28
loving relationships 8-9
lying 4, 5, 16, 18-19, 29
marriage 9
medical treatment 4
moral responsibilities 20, 26-7, 34, 36
nuclear war 39
Oklahoma City 41
older people, discrimination against 14
overfishing 43
pacifism 38
parents and step-parents 6-7
Pasko, Grigory 20
political prisoners 40
pollution 35, 43
practical action 11, 15, 23, 27, 31, 43
pregnancy 8, 9, 10
prejudice 14
the press, and invasion of privacy 16
privacy 16-17

Pro-Choice 11
Pro-Life 10
protest action 30-1
public transport 43
punishment 4, 5, 17, 24-5
racism 14, 15
recycling 43
religious principles 4, 9, 11
respect 8
retribution principle 24
right to choose 10, 11, 13, 23
road accidents 23
road building 30, 42-3
Roman Catholic Church 11
safe sex 9
scientific progress 32-3
sex 8-9
sex discrimination 14, 15
sexual morality 8
sexually transmitted diseases 9
Shipman, Dr Harold 37
social responsibility 34
soldiers 28, 29
suicide 4
surrogate mothers 33
terrorism 40-1
transplants, organ 4
trust 19
verbal or physical abuse 14
Vietnam War 28, 29
wars 28, 29, 38-9
whistleblowers 20-1
wildlife 42, 43